Usborne Naturetrail
Birdwatching

A crested tit
in winter

Usborne Naturetrail

Birdwatching

Susanna Davidson,
Sarah Courtauld and Kate Davies

Designed by
Helen Wood,
Non Figg and Laura Parker

Illustrated by
Brin Edwards, Trevor Boyer
and Ian McNee

Edited by Jane Chisholm

Consultant: Derek Niemann
Youth Editor for the
Royal Society for the Protection of Birds

Howard, the
Usborne-sponsored *Supergoose!*
(*See below for more info)

You can follow the
amazing migration of
these geese by going to the
Usborne Quicklinks Website.

Internet links

There are lots of websites with information and activities for birdwatchers.
At the Usborne Quicklinks Website we have provided links to some great
sites where you can:

- keep an online nature diary
- listen to bird calls and watch video clips of birds
- take part in surveys to help save endangered species
- find out about birdwatching events in your area
- enter competitions and win prizes
- dissect a virtual owl pellet
- meet Howard, the Usborne-sponsored *Supergoose*, and follow his
  migration from the Arctic tundra to Northern Ireland and back again.

For links to these sites, go to the Usborne Quicklinks Website at
www.usborne-quicklinks.com and enter the keywords "naturetrail birdwatching".

CONTENTS

Birds are everywhere

If you look out of a window, and look for long enough, you're sure to see a bird – even if you're in the middle of a busy city, or just looking out of a garden window. Once you start looking, it'll be hard not to see them. There are over 10,000 types, or species, of bird in the world, with new ones being discovered all the time. And you can see over 1,000 of them in Europe.

Look for blue tits, dangling like mini-acrobats on the tips of branches.

Begin at home

You don't need to go far to see exciting or exotic-looking birds. You can begin in local streets and gardens, where you might see anything from flocks of boldly painted goldfinches to summer swallows, swooping across the sky. All you need are your eyes, your ears and a little bit of patience.

If you see a little bird with a grey-brown body and a bright red breast, it's unmistakably a robin.

Sparrows flit by in a flash of whirring wings.

The secret lives of birds

Birds have dramatic and amazing lives. Cuckoos, for example, lay their eggs in other birds' nests, and leave other birds to bring up their young. The first thing a cuckoo chick does is to push other chicks from the nest.

Drab little dunnocks lurk in bushes, creeping along with mouse-like shuffles to attract as little attention as possible. But, if you catch two rival males together in spring, you'll see them performing strange "wing-waving" displays, flicking up their wings as a sign of aggression and calling loudly.

The more you look at birds, the more fascinating they become. You've started birdwatching the minute you've started to enjoy watching birds.

Blackbirds are easy to spot, with their glossy feathers and bright beaks.

Chaffinches are colourful little birds. Listen for their *"pink-pink"* calls.

You'll need to look down to see a dunnock, creeping about in the undergrowth.

Willow warbler

Garden warbler

Sedge warbler

There are lots of species of birds called warblers which look pretty much identical. Before you try to tell one warbler from another, learn to spot easy-to-identify birds, like the ones below.

Great tit

Magpie

Starting to spot

One of the brilliant things about birds is that there are so many different species. For the beginner birdwatcher this might seem a bit scary, but there is a way around it – just start off with the easy ones. Being able to tell the most basic birds apart is a good start. You probably know many more birds than you think. Try writing down all the birds you recognize and see how many you get.

Time to identify

In order to discover the names of new birds you'll need a field guide. These are books packed with pictures of birds and tips for identifying them. They are also the key to a whole new world of knowledge. Once you know a bird's name, you can find out everything else about it – where it lives, what it sounds like, where it nests and what it likes for breakfast.

There are lots of field guides to choose from. Illustrated guides are often better than those with photographs, as illustrations can show what a bird looks like more clearly. To find out how good a guide is, look up a bird you know and see if you recognize it. The best guides will also have more than one illustration of the same species. This is because even birds of the same species have different colours and patterns on their feathers.

8

Changing feathers

Taken together, a bird's feathers are known as its plumage. Males can have a different plumage from females and young birds (juveniles) can look different from adults. This is especially true for large birds, such as gulls, which can take several years to grow their adult plumage. And, just to make things even more complicated, some birds change their plumage twice a year.

But, there are ways of using your field guide that will make identifying birds a doddle (well, almost). It's to do with knowing how field guides are set out and being able to identify birds by their beaks. Find out more on the next page...

Here you can see the difference between a juvenile and an adult robin.

Adult   Juvenile

This shows the difference between black-headed gulls in summer and winter.

Summer

Winter

Compare the colouring on this male and female blackbird.

Male

Female

This ptarmigan is halfway through its plumage change. It's changing from its brown summer feathers to its white winter ones, which allow it to blend in against the snow.

These pages from a field guide show members of two bird families – warblers and finches.

HANDY HINTS

Spend time flicking through your field guide, getting familiar with bird families. It'll be a great help if you ever want to look up a bird in a hurry.

Once you're on the "owl" page of your field guide, you'll be able to identify this barn owl by its round, white face.

Using your field guide

Most field guides show birds in roughly the same order. They start off with water birds, then move onto meat-eating birds, called birds of prey, and end up with seed-eating birds such as sparrows. You'll see headings along the way, such as "ducks", "gulls", "owls" or "thrushes", that group different birds together. These groups are called "families" and contain birds that are more closely related to each other.

This makes your life a lot easier. Imagine you're out birdwatching and you see a bird with a big face, big eyes and a hooked beak. If you already know it's an owl, you can just turn to the "owl" section of your field guide to find out which kind of owl it is, rather than trawling through the whole book.

OWLS
Barn owl
Little owl
Tawny owl
Pygmy owl
Short-eared owl
Long-eared owl
Tengmalm's owl
Scops owl

Birds and their beaks

But suppose you're looking at a bird you've never seen before and you've no idea which family it belongs to. What do you do then? That's when you look at its beak, or bill.

Birds in the same family generally feed on similar food in a similar way. This means they usually have the same shape beak. While a bird's plumage can change with its age and the seasons, you can always tell a bird by its beak.

FANTASTIC FACT

The longest beak record goes to the Australian pelican. Their beaks can be up to 45cm (18in) long. They can hold more food in their beaks than in their bellies.

Chaffinch

Finches have strong, chunky beaks for cracking open the hard shells of nuts and seeds.

Whimbrel

Waders (shore birds) have narrow bills for searching for food in soft mud and sandy shores.

Mute swan

Swans, ducks and geese dabble for plants and tiny animals with their flattish bills.

Kestrel

Birds of prey, such as kestrels, eagles and hawks, use their hooked beaks for tearing strips of meat.

Grey heron

Herons, storks, grebes, cranes and terns have straight, dagger-shaped bills for catching fish.

Blackbird

The thrush family have general-purpose shaped beaks for a mixed diet of fruit, insects and worms.

KEY QUESTIONS...

...to help you identify mystery birds. Ask:

1. What size is it? Try and compare it to a bird you know.

2. What shape is it?

3. What colours are its feathers, beak and legs? Are there any striking markings?

4. How does it behave?

5. What's its call or song like?

Being a bird detective

If you're out in a field, or looking through a window, and you spot a mystery bird, the first thing to remember is to keep looking at it. (Don't reach for your field guide in a mad panic). If the bird flies away and you can't remember what it looked like, then you've scuppered your chances of ever finding out what it was. So, instead, keep your eye firmly on it and, like a detective, ask yourself questions as you look.

Then, with your answers in mind, flick through your field guide to find out your mystery bird.

Coots

Mute swans

Duck landing

Female mallard

Mystery bird

Male mallard

Making notes

Many birdwatchers carry notebooks with them to make sure they get down all the details. That way, they won't forget any vital info when they try to look up a bird later on.

As well as noting down what a bird looks like, you should also mention the date, time and place where you saw it. This will help you work out what it is. Some birds are only found in a particular type of place, or habitat, such as woods or moors. The time of year is important too, as birds come and go with the seasons.

HANDY HINTS

When you're watching birds, don't just study their appearance. Look at what they're *doing*. Note down how the bird moves and feeds, whether it's on its own or with others, or if it's out in the open or hiding in bushes.

Mystery bird?

April 6th 10.30am
Big Lake

Size - smaller than a swan but bigger than a coot

swan

?

coot

Shape - Typical duck shape!

Markings -

yellow eyes

black head with purple gloss

droopy crest

Behaviour - Diving for food in shallow water

Call - Making quiet, low whistles

Conclusion -
It's a MALE TUFTED DUCK

This is called upending.

For more information on sketching birds, turn over the page.

Birds' bits and pieces

Each part of a bird has a special name. These words often pop up in field guides and can come in handy when you're trying to describe a bird in detail. For example, you can talk about a goldfinch having a black, white and red head. But if you want to be more specific – and scientific – you should say it has a red forehead, black crown and white ear coverts.

See the picture below for more bird-words, and try to keep them in mind when taking notes.

Wing bars

Secondary feathers

Primary feathers

You can see the wing markings on this flying goldfinch, along with its long primary feathers and shorter secondaries.

FEATHERY FACT

Birds' feathers are made from a substance called keratin – which is what your nails and hair are made from too.

This shows the markings of a goldfinch.

Forehead

Crown

Beak or bill

Ear coverts

Nape

Throat

Back

Breast

Wing

Belly

Rump

Flank

Tail

Simple sketching

Some birdwatchers do simple sketches, and then add their notes around them. You don't have to be good at drawing to do this, and it can be quicker too, as all you have to do is point to the colours and markings.

Here's a step-by-step to doing a quick field sketch:

1. Draw two circles for a head and body.

2. Add a beak, neck, tail and legs.

3. Add details of feathers.

Add wings in order to sketch a bird in flight.

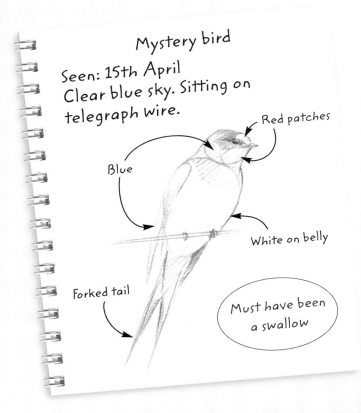

Mystery bird

Seen: 15th April
Clear blue sky. Sitting on telegraph wire.

Red patches

Blue

White on belly

Forked tail

Must have been a swallow

But if you *really* don't want to draw, then don't worry about it. Notes by themselves are just fine. You can also use signs, instead of writing out whole words, to save you time. Look at the pad on the right for some examples.

♂ = MALE
♀ = FEMALE
JUV = JUVENILE/YOUNG
(BIRD NOT IN ADULT FEATHERS)
* = NEST
C10 = ABOUT TEN (WHEN TALKING ABOUT NUMBERS OF BIRDS)

Calls and songs

You'll often hear a bird before you see it. Or you'll hear a bird and see nothing at all, if it's flying high or hiding in the undergrowth. This is where knowing a bird by its call or song comes in very handy. All birds use calls to communicate with each other, and you'll hear these throughout the year. Songs are more complicated, tuneful sounds and birds usually only sing in spring.

Winter is the best time to learn bird calls, when few birds are singing and there are fewer leaves on the trees, so birds are easier to see. Listen out for the birds below:

Blue tit
Where: woods
Call: *tsee-tsee-tsee*

Chaffinch
Where: woods & gardens
Call: *pink-pink*

Jackdaw
Where: fields
Call: *jack*

Grey heron
Where: lakes & ponds
Call: *frank* (when flying)

A robin on its song perch. Robins are one of the few birds that sing all year round.

Bird talk

To learn bird sounds, begin by trying to find the bird that's making a noise. Next time you'll connect up the bird and the sound in your head. To help make bird sounds clearer, cup your ears as you listen.

Birds have different calls to mean different things, such as alarm calls to signal danger, or calls to make contact with other birds. Watch what birds are doing as they call, to see if you can work out what their different calls mean.

Songsters and tricksters

In spring, especially at dawn and dusk, the air suddenly comes alive with birdsong. Male birds sing to attract females and to warn other birds away from their territory – the area where they nest and feed. Listen out for each new species as it comes into song.

There's no way around the fact that learning bird songs can take ages. It's like grasping a whole new language. What's worse is that some birds seem as if they're out to trick you on purpose. Listen carefully and you'll hear blackbirds impersonating alarm clocks, song thrushes imitating lawnmowers and starlings sounding like anything from buzzards to sheep and frogs.

If you hear a starling singing, you might think it's your telephone.

This list shows some of the first birds to come into song in spring. Make a list of your own and add to it.

My spring bird list:

Song thrush
1st heard: Feb 6th
Sings — very loudly!
Short, varied phrases,
repeated 2-4 times.

Great tit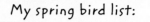
1st heard: Feb 26th
Sings — a loud and
rhythmic phrase:
tea-cher, tea-cher, tea-cher.

Blackbird
1st heard: Mar 7th
Sings — a simple series
of phrases of 2-4 fluty
notes, separated by pauses.

Chiffchaff
1st heard: Mar 25th
Sings—its name, but in a
funny order: chiff-chaff,
chaff-chiff, chaff-chiff-chiff.

Cuckoo
1st heard: Apr 18th
Sings — a far-carrying
"cuc-oo, cuc-oo". The
female has a bubbling trill.

Flying high

One of the best things about birdwatching is watching birds fly. With the help of light, hollow bones, powerful muscles and a covering of feathers, birds achieve what humans can only dream of... the ability to soar, dive, flap and zoom across the sky. Watching them can give a sense of wonder, whether it's the rapid whirring wingbeats of a sparrow, or the steep power dive of a falcon, hunting on the wing.

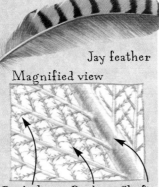

FEATHERY FACT

Birds' feathers need to form a smooth surface for flight. Barbules with hooks hold everything in place.

Jay feather

Magnified view

Barbule with hooks   Barb   Shaft

Flight styles

As you watch birds fly you'll notice that different kinds of birds fly in different ways. There are four main types of flight to look out for: flapping, gliding, soaring and hovering.

In *flapping flight*, a bird beats its wings up and down. Some birds, such as herons, flap their huge wings very slowly, while others, such as kingfishers, flap their wings so fast all you can see is a blur of blue.

Here you can see the flapping flight of a coal tit. Sparrows, tits, thrushes and warblers all have flapping flight.

18

In *gliding flight*, a bird holds out its wings stiffly to catch air currents. This allows it to stay in the air for a long time without having to waste energy flapping.

To achieve *soaring flight*, a bird holds its wings in the same way, but uses up-currents of warm air to gain height, so that it spirals upwards through the sky.

Only a very few birds use *hovering flight*, which allows them to hover in the air in one spot. They do this by angling their bodies and flapping their wings very quickly.

A kittiwake gliding

A kestrel hovering

Flight patterns

If you watch birds flying, you'll see they make a pattern in the air as they fly. This is called a flight path. Knowing a bird's flight path will help you to identify it, even if it's just a speck in the sky.

Buzzard

A buzzard's flight path - gliding, then soaring, up and up...

Great spotted woodpecker

A woodpecker's flight path – flapping, then gliding, which makes a wavy pattern.

Mallard

A mallard's flight path – mad, panicky flapping to get into the air, then fast and straight across the sky.

GLANCE GUIDE

Pointed wings for
high-speed flying

Long, narrow wings for
long-distance gliding

Broad, rounded wings
for weaving among trees

Large, wide wings for
slow gliding & soaring

Birds in flight

The shape of a bird's wing tells a story – about its way of life. Birds that spend most of their time in the air, such as swifts, swallows and falcons, have long, narrow wings. As a rule, the more pointed the wing, the faster the bird. Wide wings are for gliding and soaring at slow speeds, and birds that hunt in open spaces have the widest wings of all. Woodland birds have shorter wings for weaving among trees.

To identify birds in flight, look at the shape of the tail and wing, and for any noticeable markings, such as wing bars and patches of white. Note down whether a bird's neck is long or short, and if its feet stick out behind its tail.

Woods and gardens
If you live in the countryside, you'll have a chance of seeing all these birds from your window. Magpies, with their very long tails, are one of the easiest to spot.

Chaffinch

Blackbird

Great spotted
woodpecker

Jay

Magpie

Towns and cities

There are a surprising number of birds to see in towns. Pigeons rule the ground, but look up to catch a glimpse of gulls and crows – and, if you're lucky, a sparrowhawk.

House sparrow

Feral pigeon

Carrion crow

Black-headed gull

Sparrowhawk

Ponds, lakes and rivers

You can hear ducks, geese and swans as they fly, as well as see them – listen for their deep wingbeats. Herons are easy to spot too, with their huge wingspan and long legs.

Kingfisher

Mallard

Brent goose

Mute swan

Grey heron

FANTASTIC FACT

No one is sure how birds find their way on long migrations. It is thought they use the position of the sun and the stars and the earth's magnetic field to guide them.

Winging it

Many of the birds you see around you have come from far and wide. The swallow that flits across our summer skies would fit into the palm of your hand and weighs less than a bar of chocolate. But it has flown thousands of miles to reach Europe. Birds make these amazing journeys twice every year, to find food or breeding sites, where they can nest and bring up their young. This is called migration and the birds are known as migrants.

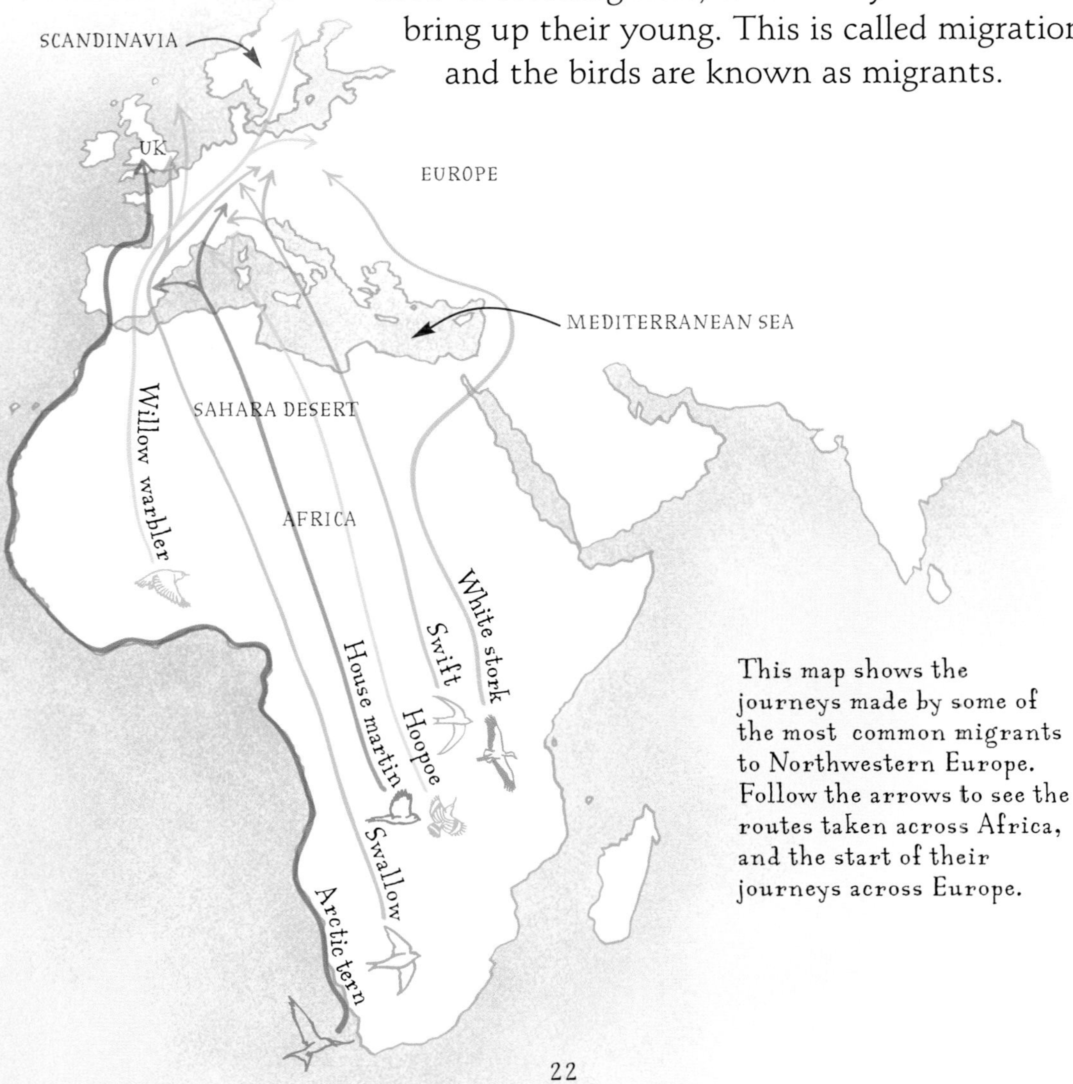

SCANDINAVIA
UK
EUROPE
MEDITERRANEAN SEA
SAHARA DESERT
AFRICA
Willow warbler
White stork
Swift
House martin
Hoopoe
Swallow
Arctic tern

This map shows the journeys made by some of the most common migrants to Northwestern Europe. Follow the arrows to see the routes taken across Africa, and the start of their journeys across Europe.

Arctic terns make one of the longest journeys. They winter in the Antarctic and some then fly all the way to the Arctic for the summer.

House martins look similar to swallows but have a white rump and a shorter tail, and are more likely to be seen in towns and cities. They arrive in Europe between mid-April and early May.

Swifts are one of the last summer migrants, arriving in mid-May. Look for them in the sky flying after insects, and listen out for their screaming cries.

Willow warblers are our commonest migrants. They arrive from mid-April to mid-May and can be seen flitting through trees.

Hoopoes are astonishingly hardy migrants. They fly over both the Sahara and the Alps, arriving in Europe in the spring. They have very broad, black and white wings, and a floppy, moth-like flight.

White storks arrive from mid-March to April. They have a gliding, soaring flight, relying on up-currents of warm air to help them on their journey.

Swallows arrive from late March onwards and stay till late summer. You can see them on telegraph wires as they gather together for the journey back.

New arrivals

Most summer migrants arrive in Europe in April or May. This makes spring an exciting time for birdwatching, as you can look out for new visitors. You could keep a record of the first and last dates you see birds through the year. Make a note of the weather too, to see if it affects when birds arrive or leave.

May 17th
Weather warm & dry.
First swifts arrive from
the south, spotted
zooming around the
rooftops.

Spring displays

As well as watching out for migrant birds, spring is also the best time to see birds showing off to each other. In order to win mates and territories to nest in, male birds sing their hearts out and make fascinating flight and feather displays. Male black grouse, for example, display together in an area known as a "lek" in order to win over admiring females.

FIGHTING FACT

Birds solve arguments in different ways. Male coots fight for females with noisy kicks, while puffins strike each other with their claws.

At dawn, the male black grouse strut around, and fan out their tail feathers.

They make "sneezing" calls and act out show fights, as females look on.

Each female then chooses the male that impresses her most.

Because male birds usually do the displaying, they tend to have more colourful feathers than the females. So if you're wondering which is a male and which is a female in a pair, you'll know the male by his brighter plumage.

You can see the gleaming red and blue feathers on this male pheasant. The females, by contrast, are a dull brown.

Songflight

Birds that live in open spaces take to the air to display, so they can be seen for miles around. Some birds combine flight displays with song. This is known as a songflight.

If you are in the countryside, look out for the mad songflight of lapwings – one of the more unusual sights of spring. They display above fields, moors and marshes, flapping crazily into the sky and rocking from side to side. Then they tumble down again, crying *"pee-wit"* as they go.

The skylark's songflight is perhaps one of the best known. The male bird rises high into the air, then hovers on fluttering wings before parachuting back down to the ground. It sings continuously in the air, with a liquid, warbling song.

Many writers have been inspired by the skylark's song. The lines below are by the famous poet, William Wordsworth.

Lapwing songflight

Skylark songflight

Snipe use a different way of claiming nesting sites. They fly high in the air, spread out their stiff tail feathers and dive steeply. The tail feathers vibrate to make a loud humming noise that says, "Keep out! This area's mine!"

TO A SKYLARK

UP with me! up with me into the clouds!
For thy song, Lark, is strong;
Up with me, up with me into the clouds!
Singing, singing,
With clouds and sky about thee ringing,
Lift me, guide me till I find
That spot which seems so to thy mind!

An osprey collecting nesting materials

The nesting season

Once the male bird has strutted and sung and paraded himself as much as he can, with any luck he will have won a mate. Then the pair have no time to waste – they must quickly build a nest, lay their eggs and raise their young. You may be lucky enough to see birds frantically flitting to and fro, searching for a good nesting spot, and then gathering material for the nest.

But, once the eggs are laid, nesting sites become trickier to spot. It is usually the female birds that sit on the eggs, and they tend to have dull plumage and markings, to match their backgrounds. This makes them hard to see. Blending into the background like this is known as camouflage. It helps birds stay hidden from other animals that could be after their eggs.

HANDY HINTS

Look out for these clues to spot nest sites:

*Birds singing from the same perch every day to mark their nest site

*Birds flying to and fro, carrying materials for nest-building

*Birds with droppings in their beaks, cleaning out their nests

*Broken eggshells on the ground – a sign that chicks have just hatched.

This reed warbler is hard to see in her nest.

Where birds nest

In the countryside, birds nest in many different places. Look out for rooks' nests in the tops of trees and swans' nests in rivers and lakes. If you walk along a river, you might be close to a kingfisher's nest without knowing it. They dig tunnels in river banks to lay their eggs.

In the city, look for crows flying up to their nests on top of church towers, sparrows flitting into crevices in old walls, or gulls simply nesting on window ledges.

Guillemots nest on cliff ledges and lay pointed eggs. If knocked, the eggs roll in circles, rather than off the cliff.

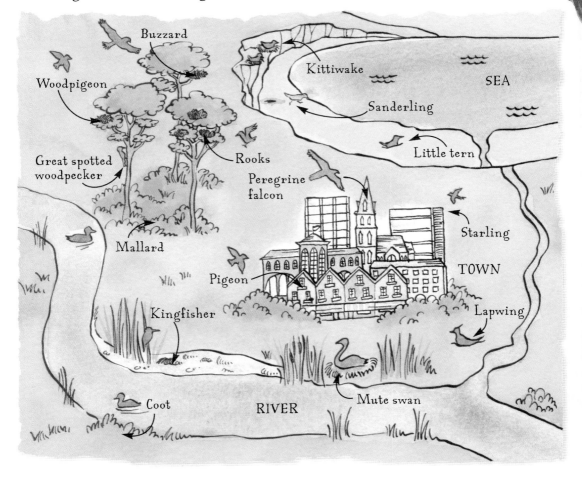

Buzzard

Woodpigeon

Kittiwake

SEA

Sanderling

Great spotted woodpecker

Rooks

Peregrine falcon

Little tern

Mallard

Pigeon

Starling

TOWN

Kingfisher

Lapwing

Coot

Mute swan

RIVER

27

This swallow is bringing food to its young. The bright red lining of their mouths shows the parents where to drop food.

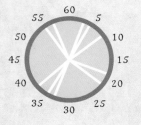

Hatching out

Birds sit on their eggs for anything from two weeks to 80 days. Larger birds usually lay the eggs that take longer to hatch. You shouldn't get too close to nesting birds: if you disturb the parents they may abandon their eggs. But, once the eggs have hatched, the fun begins – you can watch, and listen, from a safe distance.

Chicks in the nest are known as nestlings. You might hear their cheeping noises as they call for food. You can also watch the parents flying to and from the nest to feed their hungry young. Some birds make hundreds of trips. Great tits have been known to visit their nests over 600 times a day with insects.

Growing feathers

Nestlings in trees are usually born without any feathers at all, and are completely dependent on their parents. Their first feathers are soft and downy and are designed for warmth. It is only once they grow stiffer feathers that they are able to leave the nest and fly. Robins, for example, take around thirteen days to grow their flight feathers. Then their parents feed them for three more weeks while they learn to fly well. After that, they're left to fend for themselves.

A robin chick at day 1, naked and blind.

A robin chick at day 3, with its first feathers.

A robin chick at day 13, with flight feathers.

Fast learners

While some birds are born as blind pink blobs, others emerge from their eggs covered in downy feathers and ready to take care of themselves. These birds are usually ones that have been born on the ground or in floating nests on water, such as ducklings and cygnets (baby swans). They need to be active and alert, as they are very vulnerable to attack.

Mallards can swim the day they hatch, and know to dive to escape from danger.

At five days old, an oystercatcher can already run well and practice catching insects.

Shelducks quickly copy their parents and learn to sift food from the water.

A travelling circus

It's one of the most spectacular shows in Europe. It features a dazzling array of singers, sky divers, dancers and acrobats. The performers come from all over the world – from Scandinavia, Russia and even South Africa. And where is this amazing spectacle? It all takes place in back gardens and local parks. The performers are garden birds – some of the most fascinating creatures on the planet.

Garden birds are ideal birds to study as you'll get to see the same birds over and over again. You'll get to know what they look like, and what they do. But be prepared for a few surprises.

This is a nuthatch. You can tell as it's the only bird to walk headfirst down bird feeders.

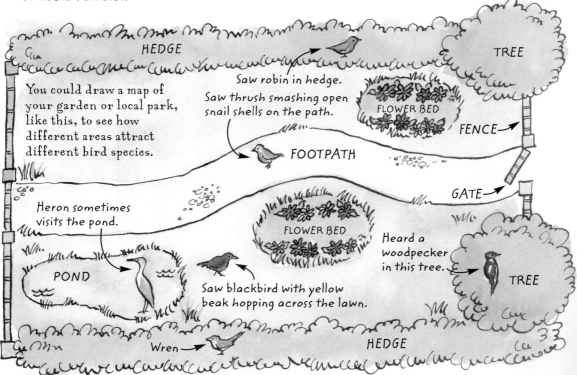

You could draw a map of your garden or local park, like this, to see how different areas attract different bird species.

HEDGE

TREE

Saw robin in hedge.
Saw thrush smashing open snail shells on the path.

FLOWER BED

FENCE→

FOOTPATH

GATE→

Heron sometimes visits the pond.

FLOWER BED

Heard a woodpecker in this tree.←

TREE

POND

Saw blackbird with yellow beak hopping across the lawn.

Wren→

HEDGE

Expect the unexpected

You might see a robin merrily singing from his perch every day. But what if another robin lands on his branch? Both birds disappear in a flurry of wings – rolling over on the ground – then flapping up together in the air. The intruder will be lucky to get away. Robins will fight fiercely to defend their territory.

Many thrushes, such as blackbirds, will squabble over mates, or viciously attack each other for a piece of food. But they do have good table manners: watch thrushes after they've eaten and you'll often see them fly up to a fence, wipe one side of their beaks on the fence, and then the other.

If you watch garden birds day in, day out, you'll soon glimpse another side to the secret lives of birds.

> ***RED ALERT***
> The colour red makes robins aggressive. They may attack anything even slightly red – from a pile of autumn leaves to a bushy ginger beard.

This blackbird and fieldfare are having a face-off to see who will get to eat the apple. If neither backs down, they will launch into a vicious fight.

BIRD FEAST

Instead of buying bird food, you could make a bird cake, using nuts, cake crumbs, oatmeal and dried fruit. Just follow the steps below.

1. Put 500g (1lb) of the ingredients into a heat-resistant bowl.

2. Melt 250g (0.5lb) of solid fat in a saucepan at a low heat. Then carefully pour the fat over the mixture, and leave it to set.

3. Turn the cake out when it's cold and put it out in the garden. Then watch the birds peck away at it.

Feed the birds

The simplest way to encourage birds to come to your garden is to feed them. Birds will eat all sorts of food – from nuts and fruit, to bacon bits and cheese. Some birds search for food on the ground, while others feed on branches of trees, so it's important to leave food out at different levels. You could wedge lumps of cheese into the bark of trees, leave seeds and nuts out on a bird table, or scatter pieces of fruit on the ground.

These birds quickly eat up the bird food scattered on the ground. Can you tell which birds they are? *

It's especially important to leave out food in winter, when birds' natural sources of food are scarce. By December fruits will have been eaten, insects are hiding away and the ground may have frozen over. Birds need lots of energy at this time, to help them to survive the cold winter nights.

*Male and female blackbird, and five greenfinches.

How to make a bird feeder

To make a bird feeder of your own, you will need a pencil, some scissors, some string and a plastic milk carton.

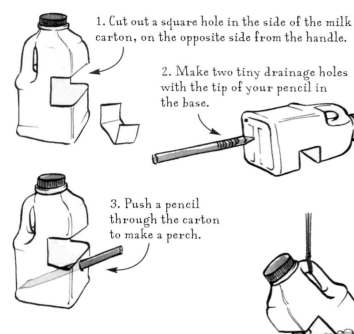

1. Cut out a square hole in the side of the milk carton, on the opposite side from the handle.

2. Make two tiny drainage holes with the tip of your pencil in the base.

3. Push a pencil through the carton to make a perch.

4. Fill the feeder with seeds. Then use the string to hang the feeder from a tree, a washing line or a bird table.

A room with a view

If you don't have a garden, you can set up a feeding station on a sheltered windowsill. You could use a window box as a feeding area. Fill it almost to the top with soil, and put the food on the surface.

HANDY HINTS

Thread peanuts in their shells on thin string, and hang them up in winter. Don't put them out in spring or summer though, as young birds can choke on them.

BIRD MENU

Do put out:

Oats

Seeds

Soaked raisins

Cheese

Cooked rice
- unsalted, as birds can't process salt

Bread
- only in winter, as young birds choke on it

~

Don't put out:

Salted peanuts

Roasted peanuts

Milk
- birds can't digest it

Cooked porridge
- it glues birds' beaks together

All these plants make good bird food.

Rowan

Ivy

Shepherd's purse

Wild grasses

Hawthorn

Thistle

A greenfinch drinks from a garden pond. Doves are the only birds that can gulp down water, so this greenfinch will have to tip back its head to swallow.

Bird gardens

Trees and bushes in gardens and parks provide food, shelter and nesting sites for birds. In the summer, lots of birds feed off fruit trees, while in the autumn, they visit gardens to pluck berries off bushes. Rowan berries, for example, attract chaffinches and siskins. Weeds, such as thistle and shepherd's purse, are especially popular with finches, which love to eat the seeds.

Thirsty birds

Birds need water too, for drinking and cleaning their feathers. Providing water is especially useful during hot, dry summers and very cold winters, when ponds and streams freeze over. If you have a garden pond, birds will drink and bathe in it. If you don't, a deep plant pot saucer can make an excellent bird bath.

Gobbling and guzzling

If you watch birds feed, you'll soon learn what food they like to eat, and how they eat it. Robins pick randomly at berries, starlings feed in large gangs, while one song thrush may viciously attack another to steal its food. Crows bury any extra food they find, disguise the hiding place, and then return later to uncover their stash.

The more you watch, the more you will learn about the different lives of birds. You could make a feeding chart to keep a record.

This blackbird is about to snap up a hawthorn berry.

Feeding Chart

Bird	Insects	Berries	Seeds	Cheese	Apples	Nuts
Blue tit	✓	✓	✓	✗	✗	✓
Dunnock	✓	✗	✓	✓	✗	✗
Blackbird	✓	✓	✗	✓	✓	✗

Observations:

Saw a sparrowhawk come in low over the garden hedge and grab a blue tit from the bird feeder. It snatched it up in its claws and flew off with it.

Later found lots of feathers scattered beneath a stump. The sparrowhawk must have plucked it first before eating it.

IN THE TREES
Blue tits and great tits will scrap over food on feeders, but they don't fight when they return to trees. They find food on different parts of the branches.

Great tits search on thicker twigs.

Lighter blue tits can hang from the thinnest, outermost twigs.

Other birds to spot on the feeder:

Long-tailed tit (see p.55)
Nuthatch (see p.55)

Birds to spot beneath the feeder:

Chaffinch (see p.38)
Dunnock (see p.38)
Fieldfare (see p.39)
Wren (see p.38)

On a bird feeder

Bird feeders are home to some of the most acrobatic garden birds. They will give you a great opportunity to see birds close up, and marvel at their gravity-defying antics as they flit, dance and peck at their food. Nuthatches strut down feeders headfirst while blue tits hang upside down on them, grasping on with their feet. Here are some of the birds you might see on your feeder.

Coal tit
11cm/4"
Looks a little like a great tit, but is smaller and less colourful. Olive grey on top, black head and white cheeks. All year round.

Blue tit
11cm/4"
Bright blue, yellow and green bird. It sometimes raises the blue feathers on its head to form a small crest. All year round.

Great tit
14cm/5.5"
The biggest European tit. It will budge blue tits away with a simple squawk. All year round.

Greenfinch
15cm/6"
The clumsy clown of the feeder. Not very acrobatic, but it still gets at the food with its large beak. All year round.

Female

Male

Summer visitors

Summer time can bring many fascinating visitors to your garden or local park. Swifts spend nearly their whole life on the wing: sleeping, eating and mating in the air. The sky is their playground – just watch as they soar gracefully overhead. You can also spot house martins high in the sky. Look for spotted flycatchers diving after insects and swallows flitting closer to the ground.

FANTASTIC FACT

Swifts are one of the few types of birds that sleep on the wing. Before dusk, swifts rise 1,000–2,000m (3,300–6,500ft) to roost in a warmer layer of air. They can hover perfectly still as they sleep.

House martin
13cm/5"

Listen out for its twittering song. Visits farmland, gardens and woodland. April to October.

Redstart
14cm/5.5"

Black face, orange rump and chest. Constantly flicks its bright red tail. Summer visitor to heaths, parks and gardens.

Spotted flycatcher
14cm/5.5"

Sits on branches, and flies out to snap up insects before returning to its perch. Woodland edges. Spring and summer.

Female

Male

Nightingale
17cm/7"

Secretive summer visitor to dense thickets and woodland. Best found by listening out for its song in May and June.

Swift
17cm/7"

Seen high in the sky above towns and countryside. Has a screaming call. May to August.

Swallow
19cm/7.5"

Its long tail feathers help it to be such an expert flyer. Visits farmland and gardens. March to October.

On the ground

As well as looking up to see birds perched in trees or flying through the air, you can also spot lots of birds by looking down. You'll see birds strutting across grassy lawns or nipping around under thickets and bushes. These birds are searching for juicy worms, spiders, slugs and other creepy crawlies to eat. Here are a few of the birds you are likely to spot on the ground.

Wren
9.5cm/3.5"
Can be found in holes and crevices in bushes, looking for spiders and insects to eat. All year round.

Marsh tit
11cm/4"
Drawn to gardens by peanuts and seeds. Particularly fond of sunflower seeds. All year round.

Robin
14cm/5.5"
Swoops down to the ground to catch insects and worms after watching from a perch. All year round.

Dunnock
14.5cm/6"
Rummages in piles of leaves to find spiders, ants and beetles. Constantly flicks its tail and wings. All year round.

Chaffinch
15cm/6"
The flamboyant male has a reddish breast, while the female has a brown breast. All year round.

Female

Male

Starling
22cm/9"
Probes into the ground with its beak to find food. Usually flies in a large flock. All year round.

Juvenile

Adult

Song thrush
23cm/9"
Hops along the grass, and then stands still, as it looks and listens for worms and other creepy crawlies to eat. All year round.

Blackbird
25cm/10"
Bright yellow beak and sleek black body. The female is brown without the eye ring. Listen out for its melodic song. All year round.

Female

Male

Fieldfare
25.5cm/10"
Blue-grey head, brown back and yellow-brown speckled breast. Visits gardens in winter to eat seeds and berries.

Mistle thrush
27cm/11"
Creamy yellow breast with large spots. Moves in long, bouncy hops. All year round.

Collared dove
30cm/12"
Distinctive black collar. Searches the ground for seeds, berries and grain. All year round.

Green woodpecker
32cm/13"
Green upper parts, red crown and moustache. Female has a black moustache. All year round.

Woodpigeon
41cm/16"
Waddles along the ground. Its distinctive call goes "*ru-hoo ru ru-hoo*". All year round.

Magpie
46cm /18"
Black and white body with glossy wings, tinged with blue, and a long tail. Its call goes "*chacker-chacker*". All year round.

FEATHERY FACT
Some birds allow ants to crawl all over them.

They probably do this because a liquid from the ants helps clean their feathers.

HANDY HINTS

Watch out for berry-
guzzling waxwings in
winter. They travel in
large flocks and
descend on bushes
and trees to feast on
berries. A single bird
can swallow up to 500
berries in a day.

These grey herons are
squabbling over food
in Regent's Park,
London.

Rarer visitors

While some birds have made gardens and
parks their home, others only ever drop in
for a visit, either when food in their usual
habitat is running low, or in search of
shelter. What birds you see will depend on
where you live.

If there are woods near your garden or
local park, you might see a goldfinch, while
if you live near fields, you may find a
jackdaw nesting in your chimney.

Larger birds, like sparrowhawks, are
passing visitors. They usually come in
search of smaller birds they can snatch up
as prey. If you live near a pond or lake, look
out for herons hunting for fish.

Rarer birds to spot

Siskin
11cm/4"

Will visit gardens if conifer trees are nearby, or if its usual food has run low. Most commonly seen in winter.

Male

Female

Goldfinch
11cm/4"

Usually lives in fields or woods. May be drawn into gardens by teasels, or by its favourite food – nyjer seeds. All year round.

Blackcap
13cm/5"

Most often seen in summer, but will also visit bird tables in winter. Found in areas with trees or shrubs.

Female   Male

Brambling
15cm/6"

Lives in woodland, but visits gardens in winter, often in flocks. Male's head is greyish-black in winter.

Female

Male

Bullfinch
15cm/6"

A very secretive bird that usually lives in woodland. Will sometimes eat from garden feeders.

Female

Male

Waxwing
17cm/7"

Pinkish-brown bird, with black eye patches. A rare winter visitor. Usually lives in woods, but will also visit gardens and parks to eat berries.

Pied & white wagtail
18cm/7"

Searches the ground for food. Its wagging tail never stops. White wagtail is found in Europe. Pied wagtail only in Britain.

White wagtail

Pied wagtail

Cuckoo
30cm/12"

Looks similar to a sparrowhawk, with its sleek body, long tail and pointed wings. Summer visitor all over Europe.

Juvenile

Adult

Jackdaw
33cm/13"

Small black crow with a grey neck. Seen in pairs or groups. Breeds in gardens with fields nearby. All year round.

This blue tit is collecting dog hair for the soft lining of its nest.

HANDY HINTS

Nest boxes with different sized holes attract different birds:

Small: 25mm/1"
Bird: blue tit

Medium: 32mm/1.3"
Bird: house sparrow

Large: 45mm/1.8"
Bird: starling

Garden nests

In spring, birds find lots of places to nest in gardens. Some use bushes, trees, ivy-covered walls or sheds. Others, such as house martins and swallows, build their nests under roofs.

Many garden birds will also use nest boxes, as the spread of towns and farms has taken over a lot of their natural nesting spots. If you put a nest box up in your garden, make sure you leave it in a quiet, sheltered place, at least 2m (6.5ft) above the ground. Fix the nest box facing north or east, out of direct sunlight.

Hairy nests

You can help birds to build nests by leaving out materials for them, such as moss, twigs, feathers and wool, which you can hang from fences or trees. Some birds also use human hair to line their nests, which might have inspired this limerick by Edward Lear.

There was an Old Man with a beard,
Who said, "It is just as I feared!
Two Owls and a Hen,
Four Larks and a Wren,
Have all built their nests in my beard!"

Inside a nest

In the autumn, when leaves fall from the trees, it's easy to see birds' nests that were hidden in the summer. By now the nests will be empty, and you could collect them for yourself.

Like a detective carefully examining evidence, you can find out a lot about birds by looking at an old nest.

!IMPORTANT!

Some birds make their nests out of mud. If you see a mud nest, don't disturb it. The same birds may return to it next year.

1. First make a note of where the nest is, and how far it is from the ground.

2. Then, wearing gloves, take down the nest, and look inside. You might find interesting things the bird has used to line its nest, such as dog or cat hair or pieces of string.

3. Now you can start to pull different materials out of the nest, using a pair of tweezers.

4. You could stick the nest materials to a piece of card, with all the other data you have gathered.

Twigs ⟶

How far has it flown?

By looking at what a nest is made of, you can sometimes tell how far a bird must have flown in order to gather the materials.

Birds in urban areas will often use strips of paper and plastic, instead of the more usual grass and leaves.

Leaves

Moss

Grass

Mute swans in flight –
easy birds to identify
with the naked eye.

Going out and about

There's a whole world of birdwatching beyond your garden or local park, just waiting to be explored. Wear light, warm clothing on birdwatching trips, and keep to dull colours, as that will make you harder to spot. Other than that, all you need is your field guide, pen and paper, and your wits.

Looking closer

Birds have good eyesight and hearing and are always on the look out for danger. So don't be surprised if you have trouble getting close to them. To avoid looking at dots in the distance, try and get your hands on a pair of binoculars.

You'll find they come in different sizes, such as 8x30 or 10x40. The first number is the magnification power: "8", for example, allows you to see a bird 8 times closer, and the second number refers to the amount of light the lenses let in. The higher the second number, the better the binoculars in low light. But they are also bigger and harder to carry, so you need to think about this when choosing them.

USING BINS

You'll need to focus a pair of binoculars, or "bins", before you can use them:

Lenses — Central wheel

Adjustable eyepiece

1. Close your right eye, then turn the left lens with the central wheel until an object comes into focus.

2. Close your left eye and look through the right lens. Make the image appear sharper using the adjustable eyepiece.

3. Don't touch the adjustable eyepiece again, just focus the central wheel when you see birds close up or far away.

A mute swan as seen through binoculars. Being able to see the extra detail makes the bird even easier to identify.

Stalking birds

It takes a bit of practice to watch birds through binoculars, and to be able to follow a bird's flight across the sky. It's often easier to find a bird, then raise the binoculars to your eyes, rather than looking for birds with your binoculars first. It also helps to keep the sun behind you, as most birds look black against a bright sky.

Even with binoculars, you need to be careful not to scare birds away. Try to camouflage your shape by standing in front of or behind a tree. Never break cover by looking over a bush or a hedge – peer around it instead. If there's no cover in sight, just keep as still and quiet as you can.

HANDY HINTS

Be careful not to trespass across other people's land, so make sure you have permission wherever you go. Don't go out alone and let an adult know where you are.

The dotted line shows an ideal stalking route to get close to birds.

Check birds at intervals as you stalk. If they seem alarmed, go no closer.

Starting point

Point chosen for close observation

Lapwings feeding

Where to look

The best places to go birdwatching are areas that offer birds lots of food and shelter. As a rule, the more varied the habitat, the more bird species you're likely to see. For this reason, places where two habitats meet, such as where woodland gives way to farmland, or where a river meets the sea, are often brilliant birdwatching sites.

Nature reserves

If you're not sure where to go, or if you've been out on a few trips and not seen many birds, try to visit your nearest nature reserve.

This is a view of a hide in a nature reserve in Norfolk, UK. There are whooper and Bewick's swans, coots, mallards and pochards.

These areas are managed to create the best conditions for wildlife and attract as many species as possible. There are usually paths to follow and signs showing which birds to look out for. Some nature reserves also have huts, known as hides, which provide birdwatchers with shelter from bad weather and great views of birds. Some hides will also have telescopes so you can get amazing close-ups.

Picky habits

As you visit different areas, you'll notice that while some birds, such as herring gulls, seem to be able to live anywhere and eat lots of different things, others are much more picky about where they live. For example, you'll only ever see crossbills where there are pine trees, as they only eat pine shoots, buds and seeds, while bitterns will only ever breed in large, wet reedbeds.

Birds like crossbills and bitterns are known as specialists. They tend to be rarer than birds that have adapted to live anywhere, especially if their habitat is under threat from farming, building or pollution. But rare birds are worth the effort – you'll get a thrill of excitement even if you just catch a glimpse of one. The key is to go birdwatching in as many different habitats as possible, so you're always discovering new birds. Here are some rare birds to look out for.

BIZARRE BEAKS

Crossbills are very strange looking birds – the tips of their beaks cross over. They use them to prise apart the scales on fir cones so they can get at the seeds inside.

Wrynecks live in open woods and parkland. They are named for the way they twist their heads when alarmed.

Bitterns only breed in reedbeds, but spend winter in well-vegetated marshes and in reeds around lakes.

Ptarmigans live on high mountain slopes, only coming below the heather line in very harsh winters.

Capercaillies are found only in old conifer woods. They are becoming very rare as much forest land is being cleared.

HANDY HINTS
Nuthatches and woodpeckers wedge nuts in crevices to hold them steady and store them. Look for half-eaten nuts in tree bark.

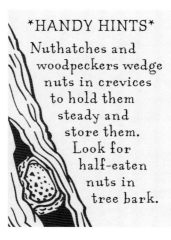

DETECTIVE WORK

Damaged feathers tell a story. A stoat will pluck a bird by biting feathers off at the base.

Birds of prey yank feathers out along the shaft.

A fox often nips feathers cleanly in two.

Bird clues

Sometimes you may not be able to see any birds, but it doesn't mean they're not there. Keep your eyes peeled for other clues, such as feathers, footprints and the remains of meals.

Hazelnut eaten by a woodpecker

Barn owl feather

Gull pellet

Look for nibbled nuts and pine cones, although these may have been eaten by small mammals.

Collect clean, undamaged feathers to build up a good collection.

Look out for pellets that birds have coughed up at feeding and nesting sites.

You're most likely to find feathers from early-spring to late-summer when birds are replacing their feathers, in a process known as moulting. You'll notice there are several different types, such as tail, wing and body feathers. Try to identify which bird they're from. You can then stick the feathers in a book.

Date:
6th September

Where found:
beach

Bird:
oystercatcher

Make two cuts in the page, 6mm apart, then thread the feather through.

Looking at pellets

Many birds swallow their food whole, then cough up the parts they can't digest, such as bones, fur, feathers and insect parts. It's hard to tell what's in most bird pellets, but by looking at owl pellets you can get an idea of what they've eaten. They can't digest bones, so their pellets may contain all the parts of a skeleton.

Feet and tracks

Birds' tracks are usually hard to find because birds are light-footed and spend little time on the ground. But you can look for tracks in snow, mud or sand. Notice the size and shape of any you find, and if the footprints are together (paired) or one after the other (alternate). Birds that walk or run make alternate tracks, and birds that hop make paired ones.

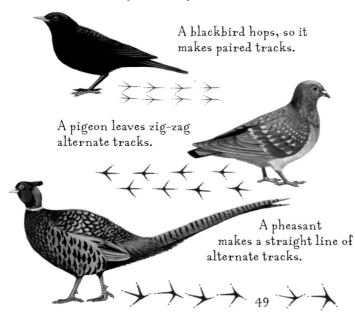

A blackbird hops, so it makes paired tracks.

A pigeon leaves zig-zag alternate tracks.

A pheasant makes a straight line of alternate tracks.

EXAMINING OWL PELLETS

1. Soak the pellet in disinfected water for an hour. Put it on newspaper, then prise it apart with sticks or needles.

2. Using tweezers, pick out tiny bones and teeth, and remove any feathers or fur.

3. Clean each part with a fine brush.

4. Try to identify any jaws, skulls or insect shells with a magnifying glass.

5. Keep your finds in boxes or stick them onto cardboard with glue & label them. Always wash your hands afterwards.

Keeping a bird diary

At the end of a birdwatching trip, even if it's just a day in the park, you can write up your notes in a bird diary, so you have a permanent record of all that you've seen.

You can stick photos, maps and feathers in your bird diary.

Robin

Curlew feather

Jay sketch

Put month & date here

3rd SEPTEMBER IN THE GARDEN
WEATHER - SUNNY AND WINDY

BIRD	HOW MANY?	WHERE?
BLUE TIT	1	ON FEEDER
HERRING GULL	5	IN SKY
JAY	1	ON GROUND

OBSERVATIONS:
Saw jay picking up acorns from the ground. It ate about five and must have been stuffing them in the food pouch in its throat. It then flew off with one acorn still in its beak. It was probably going to bury the acorns in the ground as a food store for later.

Stick in sketches too

Add bird observations

HANDY HINTS
Look up your local county bird recorder on the Internet. You can then send them your bird records, along with any sightings of rare birds.

Making records

A diary is like a detective's notebook. If you add to it year after year, noting down the birds you see, you will have a record of how the birdlife changes with the seasons. You'll also notice which birds are flourishing, and which are not. You could try to work out why some birds might be getting rarer. It could be because their habitat is getting smaller, or because of wider issues, such as global warming.

A flock of house
martins gather
together for their
journey back to Africa.

Bird casebook

Your bird diary is also your key to
unravelling the mysterious lives of birds.
If house martins nest near your home, for
example, you might note down what date
in spring you first see them swooping
overhead. Watch to see when they start
collecting mud to build their nests, and how
often they visit their young. Then look out for
the last ones in the sky as they return to Africa.

   As you read back through your diary, you'll
be able to build up a picture of birds' lives.

You could collect together your diary notes about one
species of bird, then put your notes on a separate card.

COUNTING FLOCKS

To record migrating
birds, you need to
be able to work out
flock sizes. First,
count a small
number of birds,
such as ten. Then
estimate roughly how
many groups of ten
are in the whole
flock and multiply
that number by ten.

HOUSE MARTINS

DATE	WEATHER	DETAILS
23rd April	Gloomy, cold	Saw about ten house martins in the sky.
4th May	Cold, grey	Saw house martin dipping down to muddy path in garden.
6th May	Sunny, windy	Four house martins are building nests all next to each other under the eaves on north side of house.
20th May	Rainy	House martins dart in and out of their nests all day long. Must be feeding their chicks.
10th September	Baking hot	Lots of house martins sitting up on the telegraph wires.
4th October	Overcast	All gone! I hope they find their way back next spring.

TOP TIPS FOR
SPOTTING BIRDS

1. Look for flashes of movement as birds fly from tree to tree.

2. Listen for bird calls and the drumming of the great spotted woodpecker.

3. Get up early in the spring and go down to the woods for the dawn chorus. Birds are at their most active for an hour or two after dawn.

4. Wear dark clothing so the birds won't see you.

5. Join a local bird group, so you can go on birdwatching trips to woods with experienced guides.

Woods and forests

At first, woods and forests can seem dark, silent and empty. But they're actually full of birds, making use of the plentiful food supplies of seeds, nuts, insects and small mammals. It's just that the birds aren't very easy to see. They keep themselves hidden – either from animals who want to eat them, or animals they want to eat. Birds do this with two main types of camouflage.

Jay

Disruptive camouflage –
The bird's markings break up its outline, making it hard to spot.

Woodcock

Cryptic camouflage –
The bird's colouring helps it to blend in with its surroundings.

The best place to start looking for birds is at the woodland edge, or in clearings. Fewer trees means the birds are easier to spot. Sunny patches in woods also attract insects, and insect-eating birds, such as warblers and flycatchers.

As you go deeper into a wood, keep in mind our top tips for spotting woodland birds. With a bit of cunning and practice, you'll soon be able to make out the birds from the trees.

Nesting sites

The other reason birds like woods and forests is because trees make brilliant nesting sites. Some birds nest in the branches of trees, while others nest in tree trunks. Woodpeckers make their own holes with their strong beaks. When they move out, other birds, such as pygmy owls and nuthatches, move in.

When a nuthatch moves into a nest hole, it plasters mud around the entrance to make it smaller, so other creatures can't get in.

Too-whit, too-whoo

If you're fascinated by owls, then try and go birdwatching in woods at night. It should be called birdhearing, really, as you're much more likely to hear than see an owl.

    The first thing you'll probably notice is the call of the tawny owl – *"too-whit, too-whoo!"* This call is actually made by two different owls – a female will call out *"too-whit"* and a male will answer *"too-whoo"*.

HANDY HINTS

County bird reports – available from your local library – will tell you where owls are most likely to be found, and where they roost (sleep) during the day. Keep very quiet if you visit, as owls need their sleep.

A tawny owl landing on its perch. If you can find a recording of tawny owl calls, practice imitating them. If you get it just right, an owl might answer back.

Birds to spot

Here are some pictures to help you identify common woodland birds. It also helps to know which kind of wood you're going to, so you know what kinds of birds to look out for. There are two main kinds of woodland: broadleaf and conifer. Broadleaved woods contain more species than coniferous woods, but you'll spot rare birds in coniferous woods which you won't see anywhere else.

TREE SPOTTING

Most broadleaved trees have wide, flat leaves, like these:

Oak

Common beech

Most coniferous trees have needle-like or scaly leaves, like these:

Yew

Norway spruce

Goldcrest
9cm/3.5"
Smallest European bird. Eats spiders and insects. Listen for its *"zee zee"* call. Coniferous woodland. All year round.

Chiffchaff
11cm/4"
A tiny warbler. Wags its tail as it flies. Sounds like it's saying its name. All types of woodland. Spring and summer.

Other birds to spot:

Blackbird (see p.39)
Blue tit (see p.36)
Chaffinch (see p.38)
Coal tit (see p.36)
Common buzzard (see p.71)
Great tit (see p. 36)
Green woodpecker (see p.39)
Song thrush (see p.39)
Woodcock (see p.71)

Willow warbler
11cm/ 4"
Looks so much like the chiffchaff they are best told apart by their songs. Sings a series of notes running down the scale. Edges of woodland. Spring and summer.

Treecreeper
13cm/5"
Look for a bird with a long, curved beak creeping along the trunks of trees. All types of woodland. All year round.

Nuthatch
14cm/5.5"
Sits upside down on tree trunks and under branches. Broadleaved woodland. All year round.

Long-tailed tit
14cm/5.5"
Look out for its tail, which is bigger than its body. Flies in flocks. All types of woodland. All year round.

Northern & Eastern Europe

Britain & Western Europe

Crossbill
16cm/6"
Thickset finch with sharply forked tail. Coniferous woodland. All year round.

Female

Male

Great spotted woodpecker
23cm/9"
Clings to tree trunks. Look for the red spot on its head. Broadleaved woodland. All year round.

Sparrowhawk
Male: 30cm/12"
Female: 38cm/15"
Swoops silently on smaller birds. Female bigger than male. Woodland edges. All year round.

Male

Female

Jay
32cm/12.5"
Collects and buries acorns in autumn to eat in winter. Listen for its screeching cry. Broadleaved woodland. All year round.

Long-eared owl
34cm/13"
Nocturnal, secretive owl with "ear" tufts which it raises when alarmed. Coniferous woodland. All year round.

Black woodpecker
46cm/18"
Largest European woodpecker. Found in many parts of Europe, but not in Britain. Coniferous woodland. All year round.

Red kite
62cm/24"
Bird of prey with forked tail. Lines its nest with wool and sometimes even clothes stolen from washing lines! Broadleaved woodland. All year round.

HANDY HINTS

The best time to go birdwatching is at high tide (when the water is closest to the shore). At low tide, when the water is furthest from the shore, the birds will be too far away to spot. As the tide comes in, they will move closer to you.

Estuaries

Many birds flock to estuaries – the wide, muddy channels where rivers flow into the sea. The best time to visit is during the autumn and winter, as many birds come to estuaries before flying north for the spring. There's plenty of food on offer, such as shell fish, crabs and worms that live in the mud.

How does it move?

Lots of the birds you'll spot will look quite similar, especially the long-legged waders. So don't worry if you can't tell a dunlin from a knot. Waders like oystercatchers, with their long orange-red beaks, and ringed plovers, which have robbers' masks, are much easier to identify.

You can also tell some birds apart by the way they feed. While oystercatchers pick over the surface of the mud in search of mussels and limpets, dunlins probe deeply, rapidly prodding one muddy spot, then running on to the next.

Dunlin

Oystercatcher

Ringed plover

Dunlin

Knot

Marsh harrier

Bearded tit

Brent goose

Marshes

Marshes are low, wet patches of land in which reeds grow, along with other water-loving plants. There are plenty of birds to spot in marshes all year round, but you'll have to keep very quiet and still to see them. The birds are very secretive and like to hide amongst the reeds. It's best to go on a day which isn't windy, because then you'll be able to spot birds moving in the reedbeds, and hear their songs more clearly.

The easiest birds to spot will be the ones on the edges of the reedbeds and on the tops of the reeds. You might see a bearded tit perching on the reed tops while it sings. Keep looking up too, in case a marsh harrier is flying overhead.

STRANGE SONGS

Some of the birds you'll spot in marshes don't sound like birds at all. If you think you hear a squealing pig, it will probably be a water rail, and if you think you can hear a foghorn, then there's probably a bittern nearby.

Sedge warbler

13cm/5"

Plump bird with cream eyebrows. Fattens itself up in autumn so that it can fly all the way to Africa without stopping. Marshes. Spring and summer.

Birds to spot

These pictures will help you to identify birds commonly found on estuaries and marshes. Watch out for the dramatic change in feathers in many birds from spring to winter. In spring, males have brilliant, eye-catching plumages to attract mates. In the winter, males grow dull feathers, and look much more like female birds.

Reed warbler

13cm/5"

Listen for its tuneless chattering from within a reedbed. Will sometimes perch on reed tops while it sings. Marshes. Spring and summer.

Reed bunting

15cm/6"

Will often perch upright on longish legs on tall stems. Flight jerky and erratic. Marshes. All year round.

Female

Female

Male

Bearded tit

16cm/6"

Look for its very long tail and listen for its loud "ping" call near reed beds. Marshes. All year round.

Female

Male

Dunlin

19cm/7.5"

Common wading bird. Feeds in huge flocks. Listen for its rasping "schreep" call. Estuaries. Autumn and winter.

Winter

Summer

Ringed plover

19cm/7.5"

Runs in stops and starts. Look for the black tip on its orange bill. Estuaries. All year round.

Juvenile

Adult

Adult
Summer

Turnstone

23cm/9"

Turns over stones to look for food. Makes a rattling noise. Estuaries and coasts. All year round.

Summer

Winter

Knot
25cm/10"
Larger than the dunlin.
Chestnut and black in
the summer, grey and
white in the winter.
Estuaries. Autumn and
winter.

Winter

Redshank
28cm/11"
You might see large
flocks of redshanks on
estuaries in winter. Legs
and base of bill are red.
Estuaries and marshes.
All year round.

Water rail
28cm/11"
Secretive bird - listen for
its pig-like squeal. Red
bill and pink eyes. Legs
trail as it flies. Marshes.
All year round.

Oystercatcher
43cm/17"
Black and white, with a
white collar in winter.
Makes a loud "kleep"
call. Estuaries.
All year round.

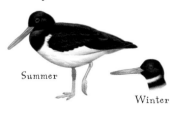

Summer

Winter

Avocet
43cm/17"
Usually seen in flocks.
Feeds by sweeping bill
sideways through water.
Estuaries and marshes.
All year round.

Marsh harrier
48-56cm/19-22"
Bird of prey which flies
slowly over marshes.
Eats small birds and
mammals. Marshes.
Spring and summer.

Brent goose
58cm/23"
Same size as a mallard.
Listen for babbling calls
from flock. Estuaries
and marshes. Autumn
and winter.

Shelduck
61cm/24"
Often in flocks. Looks
slow and heavy in flight.
Male has red knob on
its bill. Estuaries.
All year round.

Male

Female

Other birds to spot:
Black-headed gull
(see p.61)
Black tern (see p.64)
Common tern (see p.64)
Curlew (see p. 77)
Goldeneye (see p.69)
Golden plover (see p.76)
Lapwing (see p.73)
Wigeon (see p.65)
Woodcock (see p. 71)

Towns and cities

HANDY HINTS

*Look up! Many birds pass through towns when they're migrating.

*Listen out for bird calls. You might hear the "*coo-coooo-coo*" of the collared dove, chattering starlings or screaming swifts in summer.

*Look for birds in parks, in hedges, by rubbish dumps, lakes, reservoirs and canals - anywhere that provides birds with food, water and nesting places.

The black dots against the sky here are starlings, flocking into a city to roost on a winter night.

Lots of birds have adapted to living among people, and make good use of the scraps of food you spill or throw away. You'll often see pigeons pecking at bits of bread in gutters, or picking open rubbish bags to get at the food inside. This extra food comes in particularly handy in winter, when food is scarce elsewhere. Birds that usually live in the countryside sometimes come to cities to feed during the winter.

Birds make use of man-made structures to nest in, too. Sparrows shove feathers and grass into holes in roofs and buildings. Black redstarts used to nest on cliffs, but they've developed a taste for run-down buildings in towns. Jackdaws often build their homes in chimney pots, and kestrels have been known to nest on window sills. Towns are often warmer than the countryside, so some birds come to towns especially to roost at night.

Urban birds to spot

Black redstart
14cm/5.5"
Males black in summer but greyer in winter. Summer visitor but some spend the winter in the south of England.

Female

Male

House sparrow
15cm/6"
Often seen in flocks in city centres, hunting for food scraps. A huge decline in numbers recently. All year round.

Female

Male

Feral pigeon
33cm/13"
A relation of the rock dove. Colours vary from black to mottled to white. Fast and agile in flight. Very common. All year round.

Black-headed gull
37cm/14.5"
A familiar bird. Look for white front edge on wings in flight. Juveniles have duller colouring. All year round.

Winter

Carrion crow
47cm/18.5"
Often seen on their own. Call a deep harsh "caw". Thick black beak and black face, unlike the rook. All year round.

Herring gull
56cm/22"
A noisy, common gull. Listen for its loud wailing. Scavenges for food and eats almost anything. Look for red spot on its bill. All year round.

Summer

Canada goose
95cm/37"
A large noisy goose. Look in parks. All year round in Britain. Winters in Denmark and is a summer visitor to parts of northern Europe.

White stork
102cm/40"
Very rare in Britain but common in north-eastern Europe, where it nests on buildings and pylons. Summer.

Other birds to spot:
Collared dove (see p.39)
House martin (see p.37)
Jackdaw (see p.41)
Kestrel (see p.73)
Magpie (see p.39)
Peregrine falcon (see p.77)
Starling (see p.38)
Swallow (see p.37)
Swift (see p.37)

Rivers and streams

When you look at a flowing river or a babbling
brook, it's easy to forget how many thousands
of creatures there are below the surface. All
sorts of birds flock to rivers to feed on the
plants, fish, insects and worms that live there.

Some rivers have slow-moving water. These
attract swallows, house martins and sand
martins, which skim over the river, snatching
insects from above the water's surface.

Fast-moving rivers are usually found in high-
up places, flowing through rocky, mountainous
areas. It's harder to find food when the water
keeps rushing by, but the birds that live here
have adapted to hunting in these tricky
conditions. The dipper can actually walk under
water to look for food.

Kingfisher

A swallow catching
insects

Grey wagtail

A dipper searching
for food

Lakes and ponds

Most of the birds you'll see on lakes and ponds will be ducks, geese and swans. They all have webbed feet, which help them swim, and bills specially adapted to feeding under water.

Other birds you might see include herons and grebes, which both have dagger-like bills for catching fish, and moorhens and coots, which often come onto land to feed on vegetation.

Dabbling and diving

Ducks can be divided into two groups, depending on the way they feed. There are dabbling ducks, such as mallards, wigeons and shovelers, which look for food just below the surface of the water. Sometimes they upend to reach food further down. Then there are diving ducks, such as goldeneyes, tufted ducks and pochards, which swim all the way to the bottom of the water to catch food.

Shovelers

Shoveler bill

Goldeneye

Dabbling ducks sift tiny plants and animals from near the water's surface.

Hair-like teeth inside their bills trap the food, while letting the water flow through.

Diving ducks swim on the surface but dive under to feed on shrimps, insect larvae and mussels.

WEBBED FEET

Webbed feet act like paddles underwater. The webbing pushes hard against the water, helping the bird swim faster. When the bird draws its foot back, the web closes, so the foot doesn't drag and slow the bird down.

WEBBED TRACKS

Swans and ducks leave webbed tracks like this.

Coots spend time on dry land so they have partially webbed feet.

Moorhens spend most of their time on land, so they have hardly any webbing. They leave much narrower tracks.

Birds to spot

Here are birds to spot on streams, rivers, ponds and lakes. Always go slowly and quietly to the water's edge, so as not to scare birds away. Look up for gulls, terns and insect-eating birds flying overhead. If birds see you first, shy birds such as teal might fly off, while coots and grebes will dive or swim away.

Sand martin
12cm/5"

Perches on wires and branches before swooping to catch insects over the water. Digs burrows in river banks to nest in. Rivers. Spring and summer.

Common sandpiper
20cm/8"

Bobs up and down continuously when feeding and resting. Makes "*tee-wee-wee*" call. Rivers and lakes. All year round.

Black tern
24cm/9"

Black head and body, grey wings. Snatches insects from the surface of the water while flying. Lakes. Spring and summer.

Summer

Autumn

Little grebe
27cm/11"

Diving bird. Makes a whinnying sound, and disappears beneath the water when disturbed. Lakes and rivers. All year round.

Winter

Summer

Moorhen
33cm/13"

Searches for food at the water's edge. Makes a loud "*crorrk*" call. Rivers and lakes. All year round.

Common tern
34cm/13"

Hovers over water before plunging in to catch fish. Rivers and lakes. Spring and summer.

Teal
35cm/14"

Dabbles for food, filtering seeds from the mud. Mostly feeds at night when there are fewer predators. Lakes. All year round.

Female

Male

Coot
38cm/ 15"
Dives for food. Escapes from danger by running across the surface of the water. Look for white bill and forehead. Lakes. All year round.

Tufted duck
43cm/17"
Dives for food. Has a small, drooping crest on the back of its head. Lakes and slow-moving rivers. All year round.

Female   Male

Pochard
46cm/18"
Dives to feed on plants under the water. Look out for large flocks on lakes. Often asleep during the day. Lakes. All year round.

Female

Male

Wigeon
46cm/18"
Dabbling duck. Follows swans and eats plants they have pulled up from deeper water. Lakes. All year round.

Female

Male

Great crested grebe
48cm/19"
They grow their crest feathers in late winter for the breeding season. Growls and barks. Rivers and lakes. All year round.

Summer

Winter

Red-breasted
merganser 58cm/23"
Diving duck with a thin red bill for catching fish. Flies fast and low. Rivers and lakes. All year round.

Female

Male

Mallard
58cm/23"
Dabbling duck. In summer, males look very similar to females. Rivers and lakes. All year round.

Female

Male

Goosander
66cm/26"
Diving duck with a long, jagged bill (sawbill) for eating fish. Upland rivers in summer, lakes in winter.

Female

Male

Mute Swan
152cm/60"
Hisses when angry. Reaches for underwater plants with its long, curved neck. Slow-moving rivers and lakes. All year round.

Sea cliffs and seashores

The seashore has a mixture of habitats – sandy shores, shingle beaches and sea cliffs – and they all attract different birds. While sandy beaches are home to sanderlings, you'll see ringed plovers on shingle beaches, and turnstones on rocky shores. The birds you'll find by the seashore also change dramatically with the seasons – so always check your field guide first so you know which birds to expect.

Here you can see guillemots nesting together on sea cliffs. The parents fly far out to sea to find fish for their young.

Bird cities

In spring, many seabirds arrive on the coast after spending the winter at sea. Thousands of squawking birds nest together in huge colonies on sea cliffs – a stunning sight, sound (and smell!) for a birdwatcher. Each type of bird prefers to nest in a particular spot on the cliff. Puffins dig burrows on grassy slopes, while guillemots and kittiwakes prefer narrow ledges.

Living at sea

Some birds spend nearly all their lives on the waves. They survive freezing winters out on the oceans, fly through the fiercest Atlantic storms and dive deep underwater to catch fish. Known as "pelagics", these birds are brilliantly equipped for life at sea.

Diving birds, such as gannets, can torpedo into the sea from 30m (100ft) high, folding their wings just before they hit the water with a smack. Cushions of air under the skin on their head and neck protect them as they dive into the waves.

Some seabirds, such as fulmars, have long thin wings to help them fly huge distances across the oceans. Puffins have much smaller wings. They use them to propel themselves underwater, so they can swim fast enough to catch their fishy prey.

FISH BILLS

Fish-eating birds all have different types of bill, depending on the size and type of fish that they eat.

Guillemot

Gannet

Razorbill

BIRD ALERT

Some seabirds are in decline because of over-fishing. But fulmars have learnt to benefit from fishing trawlers. They follow them in huge flocks and gobble up the fish waste that the trawlers dump into the sea.

A puffin usually carries between five and ten fish in its bill. The highest recorded number was 61 sandeels.

Birds to spot

In summer, look for huge colonies of birds on even the steepest cliff faces, some of which will have come from as far away as Africa and Antarctica to breed on European coasts.

Most of the cliff-nesting birds spend the winter far out at sea, but you'll still be able to see small wading birds, such as sanderlings and knots, which come from the north to feed and wait for the spring.

Sanderling
20cm/8"

Small and energetic, with a straight black bill and black legs. Runs along the water's edge on sandy shores, where it catches tiny animals washed up by the waves. Winter.

Winter

Puffin
30cm/12"

The clown of seabirds, with its colourful bill and bright orange feet. Nests among rocks or in old rabbit burrows. Breeds from April to mid-August.

Rock dove
33cm/13"

Lives on cliffs and in quarries. Listen for its soft cooing. The feral pigeon, which lives in towns and cities, is descended from the rock dove. All year round.

Kittiwake
38cm/15"

A gull with black tipped wings. Listen out as it cries "kitti-waak". Can be seen at breeding grounds from February to August, and offshore during the autumn.

Whimbrel
40cm/16"

Large wading bird with a black stripe on its head and a long bill. Most easily found by listening out for its "pe-pe-pe-pe-pe-pe" call. Spring and autumn.

Razorbill
41cm/16"

Black upper parts and white below, with a thick black bill. Eats fish, especially sandeels and herrings. Breeds from March to July.

Guillemot
42cm/16.5"

Dark brown and white,
with a white eye ring.
Listen for its loud
whirring call. Comes to
cliffs to
breed at
huge colonies
from March
to August.

Goldeneye
46cm/18"

Look for its white and
black wing stripes in
flight. Makes a loud
"*zeee-zeee*" as part of its
display. Visits sheltered
bays and estuaries
in winter.

Female

Male

Fulmar
47cm/18.5"

Glides close to cliffs on
stiff wings. Spends much
of the year visiting
breeding sites on cliffs,
although some spend the
winter at sea.

Eider
58cm/23"

One of Europe's fastest
flying and heaviest
ducks. Usually stays close
to the shore. Breeds on
cliffs and winters in
sheltered rocky coasts
and estuaries.

Female

Male

Great black-backed gull
66cm/26"

Very large black-backed
gull with a powerful bill.
Seen on the coast all year
round. Also lives
inland during
winter.

Shag
78cm/31"

Long necked bird that
flies close to the water.
Develops a tufted crest
on its head during the
breeding season.
Winters along
rocky coasts.

Cormorant
92cm/36"

A supremely skilled
fisher. Often seen
stretching its wings out
to dry them after
swimming. Lives on
rocky shores all
year round.

Gannet
92cm/36"

Large and bright white
with black wing tips,
long neck and long
pointed beak. Best seen
in colonies on sea cliffs
from January
to September.

Other birds to spot:

Black-headed gull (p.61)
Curlew (p.77)
Dunlin (p.58)
Herring gull (p.61)
Knot (p.59)
Oystercatcher (p.59)
Peregrine falcon (p.77)
Redshank (p.59)
Ringed plover (p.58)
Turnstone (p.58)

Heathland

Heaths are good places to spot some unusual birds. Although heathland might look dry and bare, it provides perfect conditions for millions of insects to thrive in. You'll spot insect-eating birds you're less likely to see anywhere else, such as woodlarks, whinchats and hobbies.

One of the best times to visit heathland is at dusk in early summer, when woodcocks and nightjars take to the air to perform their display flights. The woodcock makes soft, croaking calls as it flies, followed by explosive sneezing sounds. Its display flight is known as "roding".

The nightjar usually flies by on ghostly, silent wings, save for the occasional wing clap. Listen for its mechanical churring trill – a sound that can echo eerily around a heath in the gathering dark.

The silhouette of a nightjar on a branch at dusk, in June. When a nightjar perches on a branch like this, it is usually a male *"churring"* to attract females.

Heathland birds to spot

Stonechat
13cm/5"

Call sounds like two stones being knocked together. Nests in gorse bushes on the ground. All year round.

Female

Male

Whinchat
13cm/5"

Look for a small streaked brown bird with white eyebrows. Perches on bushes and fences. "*tic-tic*" call. Spring and summer.

Male

Female

Linnet
13cm/5"

A sociable finch, often seen in large flocks. Linnets used to be kept as pets in cages for their beautiful song. All year round.

Female

Male

Tree pipit
15cm/6"

Nests on the ground. Sings while flying, or from a perch. Call a distinctive "*tee-zee*". Also found in woodland clearings. Spring and summer.

Red-backed shrike
17cm/7"

Preys on large insects and small birds. Stores prey by spiking it on thorns or barbed wire. Spring to autumn.

Female

Male

Nightjar
27cm/11"

Nocturnal bird. Hunts flying insects. Well camouflaged against the ground where it nests during the day. Spring and summer.

Hobby
33cm/13"

Feeds on large flying insects, especially dragonflies, and small birds. Flies with rapid wingbeats and short, fast glides. Spring and summer.

Woodcock
34cm/13"

Nocturnal bird. Hard to spot amongst dead leaves on the ground because of its cryptic camouflage. All year round.

Common buzzard
54cm/21"

Large bird of prey. Feeds on rabbits and other small mammals, and worms. Call sounds like a cat mewing. All year round.

Farmland

Everything from corn to cabbages to cattle provides rich pickings for birds. Lapwings, golden plovers and geese flock to crop fields in winter to feed on seeds and worms. Livestock attract plenty of insects, which in turn attract birds such as swallows and yellow wagtails.

But it's the edges of fields that attract the most birds – hedgerows are full of life all year round. There will be plenty of birds nesting in them in spring and early summer.

Also look out for shy partridges crouching on the ground, pheasants dashing out of hedges and sparrowhawks flying overhead.

Under threat

Modern farming methods have changed the countryside, with fewer hedgerows and a much less varied habitat for birds. This, along with the use of chemical sprays to kill insects, has meant that once common farmland birds, such as yellowhammers, skylarks and tree sparrows, are now under threat.

A yellowhammer - an increasingly rare sight. Listen for its song, easily remembered as, "*a-little-bit-of-bread-and-no-cheese.*"

Farmland birds to spot

Tree sparrow
14cm/5.5"
Smaller and shyer than the house sparrow. Often mixes with flocks of finches to feed on grain in stubble fields. All year round.

Skylark
18cm/7"
Sings while over open fields. Has a small crest which it raises when alarmed. Also found on moors and heaths. All year round.

Turtle dove
28cm/11"
Has black and brown turtle-shell pattern on its wings. Listen for its soft purring song in the summer. Spring and summer.

Lapwing
30cm/12"
Looks black and white from a distance, but has a green and purple sheen on its wings. Flocks in winter. All year round.

Grey partridge
30cm/12"
Spends most of its time on the ground, and can be confused for lumps of earth or large stones. Only flies when absolutely necessary. All year round.

Kestrel
34cm/13"
Well known for the way it hovers when hunting, especially alongside motorways. Some nest in towns. Widespread and common. All year round.

Barn owl
34cm/13"
Makes shrieking, hissing and snoring noises. Nests in barns or old trees. Hunts by flying close to the ground. All year round.

Rook
46cm/18"
Forms large nesting groups, called rookeries, in tall trees. Looks like carrion crow but has bare skin at the base of its beak. All year round.

Pheasant
Female 58cm/23"
Male 87/34"
Looks for food on the ground. Runs or flies when disturbed. Roosts in trees. All year round.

Male   Female

Moors and mountains

Wide, empty moors and steep mountain slopes are among the hardest places to go birdwatching. You can walk for hours, often blasted by wind and soaked by rain, without seeing a thing. Despite the vast expanses of land there are very few birds, as there's little food for them to eat. So why bother to look there? Well, because the birds you might see are some of the most exciting of all.

Two young peregrine falcons in a tree in the morning mist. You can tell they're juveniles as they have streaks rather than bars on their fronts.

Birds of prey

Powerful birds of prey hunt for small birds and animals over the moors and mountains. Spectacular golden eagles circle the high peaks, their amazing eyesight enabling them to spot the slightest movement on the ground far below.

Buzzards are about half the size of eagles and tend to hunt on the lower mountain slopes. From far away it can be hard to spot the difference in size, but you can tell a buzzard by its more rounded tail and wings.

If you're really lucky, you might spot a peregrine falcon – a bird famous for its ability to swoop after prey at breakneck speeds. It then delivers a death-blow with its razor-sharp talons.

FANTASTIC FACT

Peregrine falcons can spot prey on the ground from a height of 300m (984ft). When a victim is spotted, the hunter swoops down, reaching speeds of up to 180mph (290kmh).

Insect-eaters

In amongst the heather on the moors and mountain valleys are smaller birds, such as meadow pipits, as well as wheatears and ring ouzels in summer. Meadow pipits flutter up into the air in search of insects, while wheatears keep closer to the ground. They are restless birds that flirt their tails and bob up and down.

Ring ouzels are usually shy and wary. You might see them hurtling recklessly down the cliffs and over boulders in search of cover.

Breeding grounds

Gamebirds, such as grouse, live on the moors and mountains, and are shot for their meat in late summer and autumn. They spend their time crouched and camouflaged in the heather, to avoid predators such as golden eagles. But if you surprise them, they'll rocket up into the air on noisy, whirring wings, calling *"go-back, go-back, go-back"*.

In the spring, other birds come to breed on the moors and mountains. The plump-looking dotterel takes to the mountain tops, while golden plovers nest in the moors and hills.

This picture shows the different birds you can expect to see at different levels of a mountain. The birds are not drawn to scale.

!WARNING!
Be extra careful when walking on moors or mountains. It's easy to get lost and the weather changes quickly. Keep to paths and wear warm clothes.

Golden eagle

Ptarmigan

Snow line

Dotterel

Rocky areas

Buzzard

Ring ouzel

Moorland

Red grouse

Whinchat

Golden plover

Birds to spot

All these birds can be seen on moors or mountains, although most are found on the moors and lower mountain slopes, with very few living on the stark mountain peaks.

The best time to visit is in spring and summer, when birds which spend the winter on lowland fields or estuaries, come to the moorland slopes and boggy mountains valleys to breed.

Meadow pipit
15cm/6"

Most common moorland bird. Marks territory in summer by singing as it flies up into the air and then parachutes down. Upland areas in summer, lowland areas in winter.

Wheatear
15cm/6"

Nests in burrows, or among stones - sometimes in stone walls. Hovers while looking for insects to eat. Moorland. Spring and summer.

Great grey shrike
24cm/9"

Perches on bushes or trees before swooping and pouncing on small birds and voles. Sometimes hovers. Moorland. Autumn and winter.

Ring ouzel
24cm/9"

Related to the blackbird. Sings as it perches on rocks. Upland moorland and mountains. Spring and summer.

Female

Male

Golden plover
28cm/11"

Will chase each other high in the air in spring. Upland moorland in spring and summer, lowland in winter.

Summer

Winter

Ptarmigan
34cm/13"

Plump gamebird. Grey-brown in summer, white in winter. Lives on the very highest and coldest moorland and on mountains. All year round.

Winter

Autumn

Red grouse
36cm/14"

Found only in Britain. Bursts out of heather when disturbed and flies to safety before gliding back to cover. Upland moorland. All year round.

Willow grouse
36cm/14"

Lives in northern Europe. Not found in Britain. Closely related to the red grouse. Upland moorland and mountains. All year round.

Winter

Summer

Short-eared owl
37cm/14.5"

Hunts over moorland in daytime and at dusk. Nests on the ground. Lowland moorland. All year round.

Peregrine falcon
38-48cm/15-19"

Blue-grey bird of prey with a black moustache. Breeds on moorland, cliffs and mountains. All year round.

Black grouse
Female: 41cm/16"
Male: 53cm/21"

Male has a fleshy red crest over its eye known as wattle. Edges of upland moorland. All year round.

Female

Male

Curlew
48-64cm/19-25"

Nests on moors. Seen on coasts and estuaries at other times of the year. Listen for its loud, ringing "coour-li" song.

Raven
64cm/25"

Very large black bird which feeds on carrion (dead animals). Nests in high, rocky areas. Mountains. All year round.

Golden eagle
83cm/33"

Huge, solitary bird of prey. Appears dark at a distance, but close-up will show its yellowish golden crown. Moors and mountains. All year round.

Other birds to spot:
Buzzard (p.71)
Carrion crow (p.61)
Dunlin (p.58)
Mistle thrush (p.39)
Nightjar (p.71)
Skylark (p.73)
Stonechat (p.71)
Whimbrel (p.68)
Whinchat (p.71)
Wren (p.38)

Glossary

Here are some words in the book you might not know. Any word in *italics* is defined elsewhere in the glossary.

Bill Another word for a bird's beak, often used for water birds.

Bird of prey A bird with strong talons and a sharp hooked beak that hunts other animals.

Breeding season The time of year when birds build nests, mate, lay eggs and raise young.

Camouflage Body markings which help an animal to blend in with its background.

Dabbling Looking for food just below the surface of the water.

Display A pattern of movement used for communication, especially during courtship and to show aggression.

Field guide A bird identification book.

Flight feathers The long *primary* and *secondary* wing feathers used for flight.

Flight path The pattern a bird makes as it flies.

Flock A group of birds feeding or travelling together.

Gamebird A bird that is hunted for its meat.

Gliding flight A smooth flight in which wings are held stiffly to catch air currents.

Habitat A type of place where a group of animals or plants lives.

Hovering flight Flying to stay in one place by quickly moving wings in a non-stop figure-of-eight.

Juvenile A young bird in full *plumage*. A bird's juvenile plumage is often different from its adult plumage.

Migration The movement of some species from one area to another at certain times of year.

Moulting The process of shedding and replacing feathers.

Nestling A baby bird in a nest that cannot fly.

Pellet A compact parcel of undigested food that has been regurgitated.

Perch A resting place above ground on which a bird lands or *roosts*.

Plumage All of a bird's feathers.

Predator An animal that hunts and kills other animals for food.

Prey An animal hunted by other animals for food.

Primary One of the large outer wing feathers.

Reed A tall grass that grows in shallow water.

Roost A place where a bird sleeps.

Secondary One of the inner wing feathers.

Shaft The central part of a feather.

Soaring flight A way of flying that uses up-currents of warm air to gain height.

Species A type of plant or animal that breeds with others of its kind and can produce young.

Territory An area occupied by a bird or groups of birds.

Upending Feeding by tipping upside down, so a bird's head is below the surface of the water and its tail is in the air.

Wader One of a group of birds that live close to water and use their long legs for wading in search of food.

Webbed feet Feet which have a layer of skin stretched between the toes.

Wing bar A natural mark across a group of feathers on a bird's wing.

Index

79

Acknowledgements

Every effort has been made to trace the copyright holders of material in this book. If any rights have been omitted, the publishers offer to rectify this in any subsequent editions following notification. The publishers are grateful to the following organisations and individuals for their permission to reproduce material
(t = top, m = middle, b = bottom, l = left, r = right):

Cover © STUART ANTHONY SILVER; **p2-3** (t) © David Tipling (rspb-images.com); **p4** © Johan Oli Hilmansson; **p9** (b) © Michael Quinton/Minden Pictures/FLPA; **p10** (b) © Mark Hamblin (rspb-images.com); **p16** (m) © NHPA/STEPHEN DALTON; **p17** (b) © NHPA/WILLIAM PATON; **p18** (b) © Warren Photographic; **p24** (bl) © Terry Andrewartha / naturepl.com; **p26** (tl) © Frank Lane Picture Agency/CORBIS, (b) © George Reszeter, Ardea London Ltd; **p28** (tl) © Warren Photographic; **p29** (br) © Bob Glover (rspb-images.com); **p30** (tl) © Warren Photographic; **p31** (b) © Kim Taylor / naturepl.com; **p32** (m) © NHPA/ MANFRED DANEGGER; **p34** (b) © Mike Read (rspb-images.com); **p35** (tr) © Warren Photographic; **p40** © Georgette Douwma / naturepl.com; **p42** (tl) © John Daniels, Ardea London Ltd; **p43** (m) © STOCKPHOTO / Alamy; **p44** (b) © Duncan Usher, Ardea London Ltd; **p46** (b) © NHPA/ALAN WILLIAMS; **p47** (mr) © Worldwide Picture Library / Alamy; **p50** (tl) © STUART ANTHONY SILVER; **p51** (tr) © van hilversum / Alamy; **p53** (b) © Kim Taylor / naturepl.com; **p60** (b) © Wayne Hutchinson/FLPA; **p66** (l) © Steve Packham / naturepl.com; **p67** (b) © Solvin Zankl / naturepl.com; **p70** © Gary K Smith/FLPA; **p72** (b) © Dietmar Nill / naturepl.com; **p74** (tl) © Jorma Luhta / naturepl.com.

Additional designs by Tom Lalonde, Brenda Cole, Hannah Ahmed and Stella Baggot

Additional illustrations by Ian Jackson

Digital manipulation by John Russell and Nick Wakeford